Red coral, an iconic native species of the Mediterranean, brings together worlds that seem very far apart: it has long been a source of fascination for people and for thousands of years they have used it to make jewelry, works of art, talismans, and currency. It captivates the divers who discover it in its natural environment, carpeting caves in a swathe of ruby punctuated by beautiful white polyps, their small bodies moving in the currents. Our interest in red coral began long ago. It has earned it the name "precious coral."

It took researchers a long time to understand its true nature, and even today there are still many unanswered questions about this surprising creature.

And that's when Science and Art come together…

The Monaco Scientific Center, an internationally renowned research laboratory, has partnered with the prestigious House of Chanel to set up a Research Unit on the Biology of Precious Corals. They have two aims: to make important new discoveries about the key biological processes of this curious species, and to come up with innovative ways to protect it against the threats posed by climate change and intensive poaching.

It is in this context that the Monaco Scientific Center and Chanel wanted to publish this book, to raise awareness among young people about the ancient beauty of red coral.

Its publication, a hundred years after the birth of my father, Prince Rainier III, is the perfect tribute to him because, among his many conservation initiatives, he founded the marine reserve of Spélugues, which protects the unique coral drop-off in our Principality.

I am honored to introduce this book and I hope that it will more than fulfil its aim.

The Princess of Hanover

ANNE JANKELIOWITCH

STÉPHANE KIEHL

THE MYSTERIES OF
RED CORAL

MY ADVENTURE AROUND
THE MEDITERRANEAN

〜〜〜〜〜〜〜〜〜〜

Based on an original idea by Nathalie Técher,
Carine Le Goff, and Romie Tignat.

THAT SUMMER...

When I arrived at Granny's house for the summer break, I had no idea what I would find. As usual, I ran up to the attic to play. But everything had changed. Granny had decided to sort through her old boxes. I spotted a small glass cabinet that I didn't recognize. My grandma must have put it there so she could use it to store the things she'd unpacked. When I walked over, I saw it straight away. It was right at my eye level: a strange kind of colored rock with an unusual shape... like a branch. I opened the cabinet and took it out. It was very hard, completely red, and fit in the palm of my hand. But most of all, it seemed somehow magical...

I ran down the stairs and showed Granny what I'd found, bombarding her with questions. She smiled and took it from me, lifted it up, and looked at it from every angle, turning it toward the light. "Well?" I asked, impatient. Granny gave me a mischievous smile and said that, as we were on summer break, that afternoon we would go visit her friend Henri, who was a historian. He would be delighted to meet me and would explain where the object came from. "He was the one who gave it to me," Granny went on, mysteriously. "It's very valuable. It's called 'red coral'."

Asking an expert to answer my questions? It was a dream come true! I hurried to fetch my notebook and pen. I was ready to set out on an investigation and solve the mystery of the stone branch. I had a feeling that the adventure would not end with Henri...

NAME: HENRI

JOB: HISTORIAN, SPECIALIZING IN RED CORAL

LOCATION: MARSEILLES

USES, BELIEFS, AND MYTHS IN **THE ANCIENT WORLD**

? WHY IS RED CORAL SO VALUABLE?

The main reason is its color. For thousands of years, red coral has been highly prized and used in many different ways. It is a symbol of the history and culture of the Mediterranean, where it is mainly found, but it was traded as far afield as India, China, and Africa, in exchange for silk, spices, and diamonds. In ancient times and throughout the Middle Ages, Marseilles was the red coral capital of the world!

WHAT WAS IT USED FOR?

In ancient Greece and Rome, it was used for sculptures or as a precious stone. For centuries, people used it to make amulets—small good-luck charms. It was very important to Christians because of its color, which symbolized the blood of Christ. People believed it could protect boats from being struck by lightning, bring good harvests, and keep the devil away. Merchants kept a piece in their purses to bring them riches. Parents placed red coral pendants around their children's necks to protect them from illness and danger.
And it has always been used to make works of art and jewelry (see p. 40). It was called "the red gold" of the Mediterranean.

SO IT HAS MAGICAL POWERS?

Yes, in some ways! Its hardness was seen as a symbol of strength and good health. It was ground into powder and used in pharmaceutical remedies for various diseases, or in beauty creams and toothpaste. It is still used today as a homeopathic remedy.

WHERE DOES IT COME FROM?

The sea! According to a Greek myth, it first appeared after a terrible battle. You must have heard of Medusa, who had the power to change everything she looked at into stone? When the hero Perseus cut off her head, he laid it on a bed of seaweed. The blood that spilled from her neck turned the seaweed to stone. That was how red coral first came to be, and then it spread across the waves of the Mediterranean... That was the story, at least. But scientists might disagree!

A PUZZLE FOR
SCIENTISTS

IS CORAL A ROCK?

That's what people believed at first. They thought that red coral was a kind of mineral. Then, in ancient Greece and up until the 17th century, people thought coral was a type of seaweed that hardened and turned to stone when it came into contact with air. A kind of stony plant.

SO IT'S A PLANT?

In the early 18th century, Count Marsili, a keen natural scientist, did a series of experiments here in Marseilles. He found that when coral was placed in a bowl of seawater, it bloomed like a plant. He thought this proved it was a kind of plant, and many learned people, such as René-Antoine Ferchault de Réaumur, celebrated his discovery. But Jean-André Peyssonnel, a young doctor from Marseilles, was not convinced. He repeated Marsili's experiments and published his findings in England, because the French Academy of Sciences refused to accept them: he believed the white flowers that bloomed on the branches of the coral were tiny insects, like mini octopuses.

SO IT'S AN ANIMAL?

In 1727, Réaumur didn't believe a word of it! But later discoveries proved that Peyssonnel was right, and Réaumur sent him a letter to apologize. In 1742, the Academy of Sciences finally accepted that red coral was part of the animal kingdom. In 1860, Henri de Lacaze-Duthiers, a respected zoologist specializing in marine animals, studied coral more closely and set out the first scientific findings about the anatomy and reproduction process of red coral (see p. 20 and 24).

HENRI
DE LACAZE-DUTHIERS

JEAN-ANDRÉ PEYSSONNEL

Today, we know a lot more about this small sea creature. Red coral grows in plenty of places in the Mediterranean Sea, such as in Spain, in Cadaqués. My nephew Guillaume runs a diving club there. He often takes his clients to admire the coral growing under the sea. **Go and visit him, and he'll tell you where to find it!** ▶

NAME: GUILLAUME
JOB: MANAGER
OF A DIVING CLUB
LOCATION: CADAQUÉS, SPAIN

A SHY
SPECIES

? IF I GO DIVING WITH YOU, WILL I BE ABLE TO SEE RED CORAL?

Red coral can be found in shallow waters, but it prefers to live at depths of between 30 meters and 300 meters below the surface. You mustn't forget to bring a torch to light up dark corners, as that's where it likes to grow! Its favorite habitats are rocky areas, dark caverns, and in the shadow of overhangs or canyons.

DOES IT HAVE ANY OTHER PREFERENCES?

Red coral always grows in places with good water flow. Because it is attached to rocks, it relies on currents to bring it food (see p. 21). It also needs fairly cool water, between 15 and 18°C (59 and 64°F) on average. It can't survive in water temperatures over 25°C (77°F) for longer than a few days.

DOES IT GROW ANYWHERE ELSE OTHER THAN THE MEDITERRANEAN?

Red coral is mostly found in the Mediterranean Sea. You can find it all over the central and Western parts of the Mediterranean: Spain, the south of France, Corsica, Italy, Sardinia, Sicily, Greece, Algeria, Tunisia and Morocco. However, it has also spread beyond that, to the nearby Atlantic coast, from southern Portugal to Cape Verde.

You may have heard people talking about other types of coral, like tropical coral. The name "coral" covers lots of species, and some are very different from red coral. **Go and see my friend Denis in Nice. He's a taxonomist who specializes in corals. He'll show you all the different kinds!** ▶

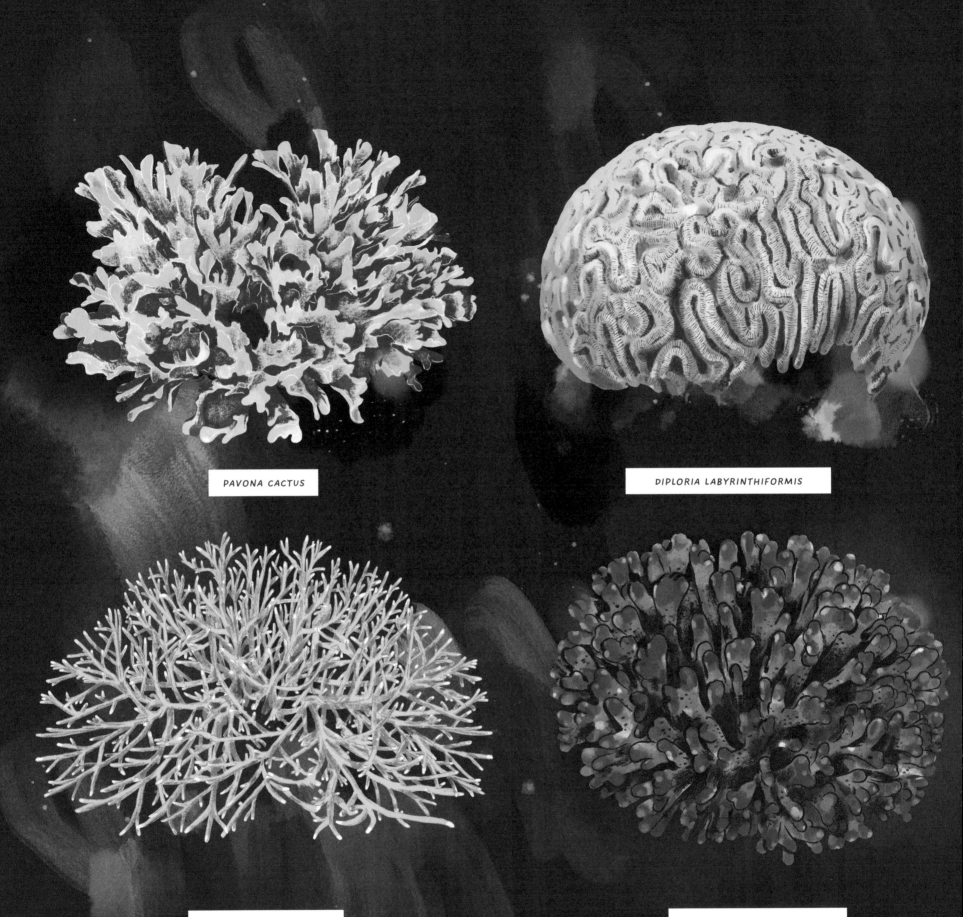

PAVONA CACTUS

DIPLORIA LABYRINTHIFORMIS

ACROPORA MURICATA

STYLOPHORA PISTILLATA

PORITES DENSA

PACHYSERIS SPECIOSA

TURBINARIA BIFRONS

LITHOPHYLLON CONCINNA

NAME: DENIS
JOB: TAXONOMIST, SPECIALIZING IN CORALS
LOCATION: NICE

A WORLD OF CORALS

? WHAT DOES A TAXONOMIST DO?

A taxonomist is a natural scientist who specializes in classifying living things. This means naming all the different species that have been identified and organizing them into categories, which are like the different branches of a big family tree.

WHAT BRANCH DOES RED CORAL BELONG TO?

It is part of the cnidaria branch. This includes lots of different animals, ranging from jellyfish and gorgonians to sea anemones and corals. There are more than 10,000 species in this group. Their name comes from the Greek word knide, which means "nettle," because, like nettles, most members of the cnidaria family can sting you! Within the corals, the *Corallium* genus includes a few species called "precious corals." This is where red coral belongs. Its scientific name is *Corallium rubrum* (in Latin, *rubrum* means "red").

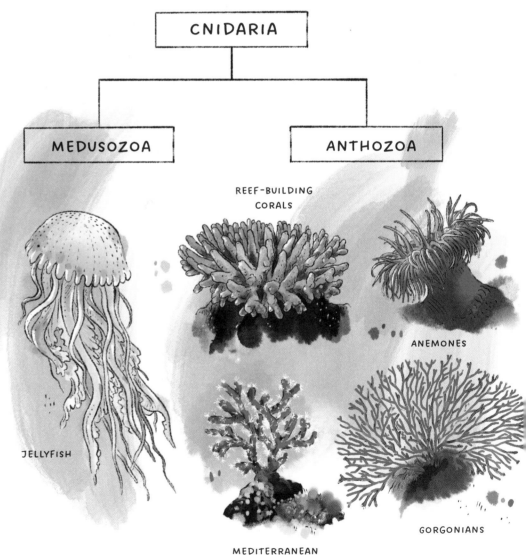

CNIDARIA

MEDUSOZOA

ANTHOZOA

REEF-BUILDING CORALS

ANEMONES

JELLYFISH

MEDITERRANEAN RED CORAL – *RUBRUM*

GORGONIANS

PINK CORAL — *ELATIUS*

WHITE CORAL — *KONOJOI*

JAPANESE RED CORAL — *JAPONICUM*

GOLD CORAL SKELETON

BLACK CORAL — *ANTIPATHARIA*

GOLD CORAL — *GERARDIA*

BLACK CORAL SKELETON

BLUE CORAL — *HELIOPORA COERULEA*

WHAT ARE THE OTHER KINDS OF PRECIOUS CORAL?

Corallium rubrum has a few close relatives: precious red, pink or white corals found in Asia, which are also used to make jewelry (see p. 40). They live at depths of around 1,500 meters, sometimes even deeper, in the Pacific Ocean off the south coast of Japan. The largest specimen, found in 2006, measured 1 meter across and weighed more than 60 kg (130 lb)! Black, blue and gold corals are called semi-precious, and are also cousins of red coral.

HOW ARE TROPICAL CORALS DIFFERENT?

They belong to different groups. We call them "reef-building corals" and they are found in tropical and subtropical waters, for example on the Great Barrier Reef in Australia. They come in many different shapes—branching, spherical, or flat and plate-like (see p. 16–17)—and they provide a habitat for lots of different animals and plants. Unlike red corals (from the *Corallium* family), they often host microscopic algae which provide them with the food and oxygen that they need. Because the coral and algae both benefit from this, it is called a symbiotic relationship. The algae need light and these tropical corals are usually found in shallower, warmer waters than red coral!

Would you like to know how red coral grows and feeds itself, without this symbiotic relationship? **Go and see Nathalie. She's a biologist at the Monaco Scientific Center and is very interested in this unusual animal.** ▶

AN UNUSUAL LITTLE ANIMAL

NAME: NATHALIE
JOB: BIOLOGIST
LOCATION: MONACO SCIENTIFIC CENTER

? CORAL DOESN'T LOOK MUCH LIKE AN ANIMAL!

You're probably thinking of the animals that you know! It's true that coral looks very different, because it doesn't have eyes, legs, or fins, and it doesn't move around. However, like the animals you know, it eats other living organisms. And when we look at it more closely, we can see that it is actually a colony of hundreds of tiny moving creatures, called "polyps." These are joined together by a kind of skin, or "tissue," which covers a hard, branch-shaped structure, the skeleton. This shared skeleton supports the whole colony (see p. 22).

A: RETRACTED POLYP   B: EXTENDED POLYP   C: TISSUE   D: SKELETON

WHAT DO POLYPS LOOK LIKE?

They are the small white shapes that you can see
moving on the surface of branches of coral,
that look like mini anemones. They are no larger
than 5 millimeters and their sac-like body has eight
tentacles at the top and only one opening, which
functions as both their mouth and their anus.
Inside the sac is their gastrovascular cavity—a bit
like a stomach.

WHAT DO THEY EAT?

Polyps are carnivorous and they eat plankton—
microscopic marine organisms that drift on
the current—as well as food particles that have
dissolved in the sea. As they can't move, polyps
use their tentacles, which are fringed with tiny
projections called "pinnules." These form a kind
of sieve that filters the water and catches the tiny
prey that pass through on the current... The tentacles
also have cells that hide a formidable weapon: a tiny
harpoon which springs out at the slightest touch
and injects its prey with venom that paralyzes it.
Then all the polyp has to do is bring the prey to
its mouth and digest it.

E: PLANKTON VIEWED THROUGH A MICROSCOPE

F: PLANKTON   G: PINNULE

H: TENTACLE   I: MOUTH

THE CORAL'S SKELETON, AN **EXTRAORDINARY MATERIAL**

IS THIS SKELETON LIKE OUR BONES?

Red coral produces a cylindrical, branching skeleton (see p. 20) made of calcium carbonate, which is attached to the rock and supports the entire colony. Other animals and plants produce mineral structures, called biominerals, in the same way. You already know some of them: snails' shells, shellfish and eggshells, for example, but also human teeth and bones.

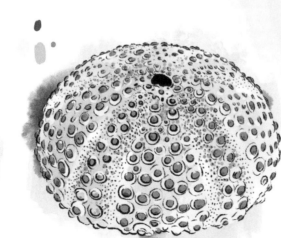

HOW IS IT MADE?

Coral needs calcium to make its skeleton, just as we do to make our bones. It absorbs this from sea water, then transforms it into calcium carbonate, by a process called "calcification." This is how the skeleton's axis grows both longer and wider. You can see the growth ridges in coral when you cut it open. They look like the growth rings in a tree! Coral also produces lots of tiny grains of calcium carbonate, called "spicules," which are found throughout its tissue. They are thought to make the red coral colony more sturdy.

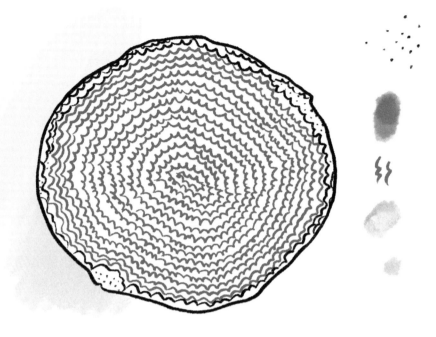

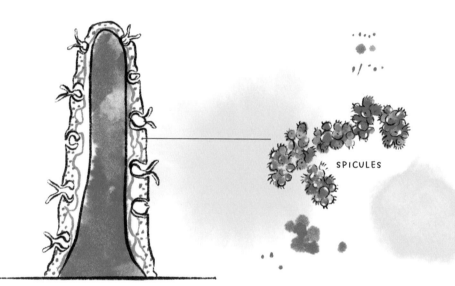

SPICULES

DOES THE SKELETON EVER BREAK?

It is very tough. Like all biominerals, it is built around a kind of frame made from organic matter. This means it is like reinforced concrete, where the concrete is the calcium carbonate and the steel bars are the frame, or "matrix." The matrix plays a role in the calcification process and makes the biomineral very sturdy.

IS THE SKELETON WHAT PEOPLE USE TO MAKE JEWELRY?

Yes! As well as being very hard, it has a pretty red color, which doesn't fade even when it's taken out of the water. This is due to a natural pigment that comes from the same family as carotene, which is found in carrots and tomatoes! It can turn the skeleton different shades, from bright red to pale pink. There are even albino red corals, which are completely white because they don't have any pigment!

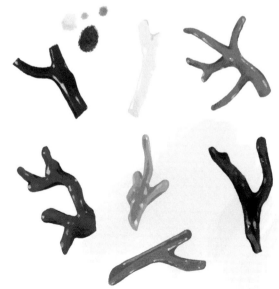

LIVING WITHOUT MOVING AROUND

DOES RED CORAL HAVE ANY ENEMIES?

It has a few predators, such as grazing fish, a small gastropod, and boring sponges. So the red coral has to defend itself, although it can't move! The polyps can retract into a small cavity inside the tissue. The spicules (see p. 23) are also not very appetizing to grazing fish. The coral can produce mucus (a slimy liquid) to ward off intrusive neighbors. And if that doesn't work, it has tentacles that can sting!

HOW DOES RED CORAL REPRODUCE?

A colony is made up of either all male or all female polyps. A male polyp can start reproducing a year after it's born, while a female polyp has to wait two years. As they can't move, the polyps can't mate! So, in summer, the male colonies release sperm cells into the water, and these swim toward the female colonies. The eggs are fertilized and then develop for around a month in the female polyp's gastrovascular cavity. This is called sexual reproduction.

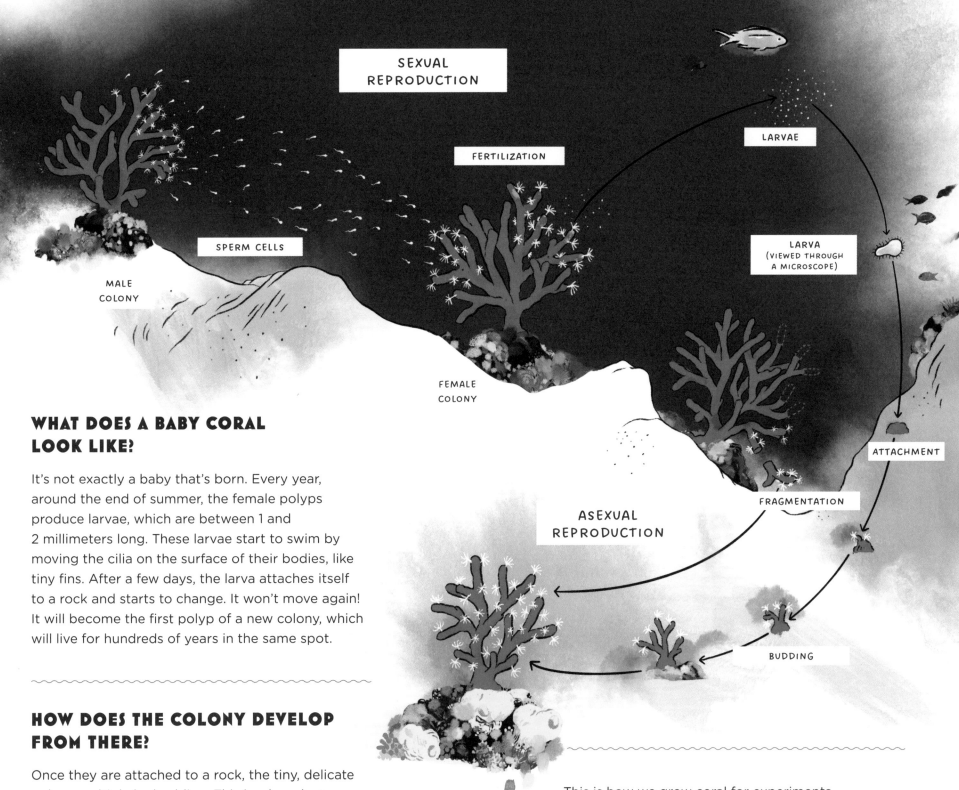

SEXUAL
REPRODUCTION

FERTILIZATION

LARVAE

SPERM CELLS

LARVA
(VIEWED THROUGH
A MICROSCOPE)

MALE
COLONY

FEMALE
COLONY

ATTACHMENT

FRAGMENTATION

ASEXUAL
REPRODUCTION

BUDDING

WHAT DOES A BABY CORAL LOOK LIKE?

It's not exactly a baby that's born. Every year, around the end of summer, the female polyps produce larvae, which are between 1 and 2 millimeters long. These larvae start to swim by moving the cilia on the surface of their bodies, like tiny fins. After a few days, the larva attaches itself to a rock and starts to change. It won't move again! It will become the first polyp of a new colony, which will live for hundreds of years in the same spot.

HOW DOES THE COLONY DEVELOP FROM THERE?

Once they are attached to a rock, the tiny, delicate polyps multiply by budding. This is why, when a sea creature or a storm breaks off part of the coral, it doesn't die. That part can attach itself to another rock and carry on developing, like a cutting taken from a plant! This is called "asexual" reproduction because the polyp doesn't need to be fertilized by a polyp of the opposite sex.

This is how we grow coral for experiments. There are a lot of things about coral that we're still trying to understand. **My colleague Stéphanie has been growing red coral in artificial caves for many years. Go and see her, and she'll tell you why!** ▶

GROWING CORAL

NAME: STÉPHANIE
JOB: RESEARCH BIOLOGIST
LOCATION: MONACO
SCIENTIFIC CENTER

? IS IT TRUE THAT WE KNOW HOW TO GROW CORAL?

We have done some experiments to find out. As coral can reproduce by budding, we have tried to grow it in its natural environment. In 1989, scientists submerged four artificial caves in an underwater reserve near Monaco, at a depth of 40 meters. The caves were concrete cubes, big enough for divers to swim inside, attach pieces of coral and come back regularly to observe them. The coral cuttings survived very well on their artificial rocks and they even carried on reproducing: two years later, there were small new colonies on the ceiling!

ARE THERE STILL EXPERIMENTS BEING CARRIED OUT TODAY?

There has recently been a new experiment. In July 2021 researchers at the Monaco Scientific Center submerged six new caves in order to determine the best conditions for reproduction.
This method allowed them to catch some of the larvae, which attached themselves to the caves, and observe their development.

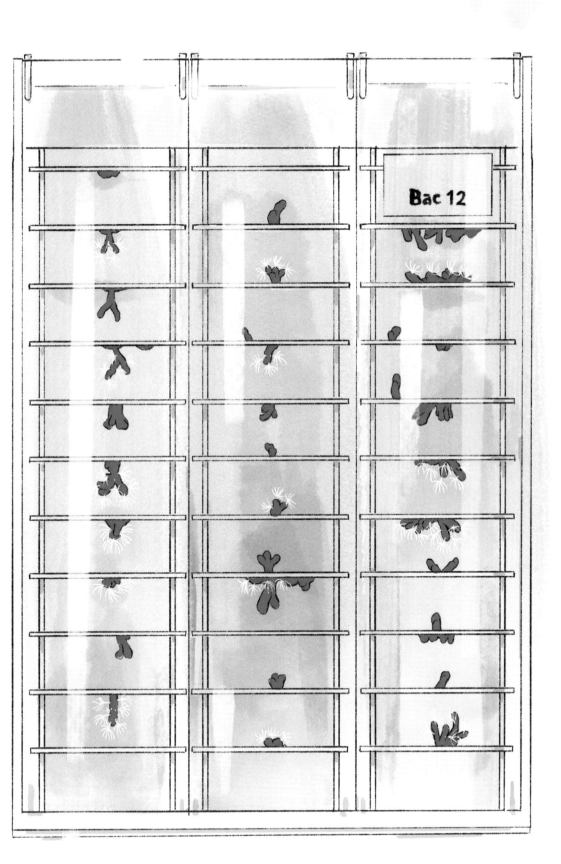

Bac 12

CAN CORAL ALSO SURVIVE IN AN AQUARIUM?

It's only possible in controlled conditions, in a research lab, if you feed plankton to the cuttings. The advantage of this method is that you can vary the current, temperature, and acidity of the water, and record what happens as a result. This allows scientists to determine the best conditions for reproduction, for larvae to survive and attach themselves to a rock, and for colonies to grow.

DOES CORAL GROW QUICKLY?

It depends on where it is, how much plankton there is, and what the current is like, as that affects the coral's shape: the stormier the current, the bushier the colony. But it always grows slowly: it can grow between 2 and 10 millimeters in length per year, and a branch's diameter can increase by 1/2 millimeter! A colony that weighs a few grams might be around 20 years old. The largest colonies are many centuries old (see p. 19)! You might think that being able to grow coral would allow us to repopulate the natural habitats that have been damaged, but that would take far too long. It would be much better to look after the colonies that already exist!

If you want to know more about the health of the red coral population in the Mediterranean, **go to the harbor and see Jérémie on the boat *Eleuthera*. He's one of my research students. He's just come back from a marine science trip to North Africa!** ▶

NAME: JÉRÉMIE
JOB: RESEARCH STUDENT
LOCATION: RESEARCH SHIP
ELEUTHERA

THE RED CORAL **POPULATION** IN THE MEDITERRANEAN

WHAT HAPPENS ON A RESEARCH SHIP?

There is a research lab on board with instruments for taking measurements and readings as well as taking and analyzing samples, diving equipment, and sometimes a remote-operated robot or a mini-submarine for working at low depths. As well as the crew, there are scientists on the ship who study the marine environment or a particular species. They observe how it lives or how its population changes. It's easier to do that when you're on location!

IS RED CORAL DISAPPEARING?

Research has shown that coral populations at depths of less than 50 meters—the ones that are easiest to reach for harvesting—are declining. Even though red coral reproduces well, new corals grow too slowly to quickly replenish stocks in places where it's been harvested. In these shallower waters, there is nothing left except for a few young branches. Large colonies, which attracted coral harvesters, have become rare. You have to go deeper to find them.

CAN WE COUNT ALL CORALS?

To be honest, we can't count them one by one! What we can tell from our observations is that the red coral population in the Mediterranean is divided into different "spots" and the colonies are more or less dense depending on their exposure to currents and the depth at which they live. We use the mini-submarine to take photos of colonies, measure them, and estimate their numbers, then we go back to the same spot a few years later to compare what we see. When it comes to analyzing how the populations develop over the years, the problem is that there were no studies of coral populations before we started to exploit them!

As well as harvesting, there are other serious threats to the future of red coral. **Go and see Lorenzo, the director of the Cerbère-Banyuls Marine Nature Reserve, which is home to a protected red coral population, and he'll tell you about them.** ▶

NAME: LORENZO
JOB: DIRECTOR
LOCATION: CERBÈRE-BANYULS
MARINE NATURE RESERVE

GROWING
THREATS

? WHAT CAN KILL RED CORAL?

Coral harvesting is now strictly regulated
(see p. 38) to reduce the amount of coral being
removed from the sea, but there are poachers
who ignore the rules and continue to illegally fish
for coral. Red coral is also threatened by chemical
pollution and sediment (for example, in muddy
water), which smothers it.

IS CORAL AFFECTED BY CLIMATE CHANGE?

Over the last few years, we have had a few especially hot summers and we've seen higher mortality rates in red coral, especially in shallow waters. We know why: it can't survive very long in water that is too warm! Global warming will most likely make this problem worse. In the longer term, toward the end of this century, there will be another threat to the survival of red coral: ocean acidification. Red coral won't like that either!

CORAL SKELETON
DAMAGED BY HEAT

WOULD CORAL LIVE FOREVER IF HUMANS DIDN'T INTERFERE?

The colonies would probably grow larger, in line with their age, if humans didn't harvest them! But coral also has natural predators (see p. 24), such as a "boring" sponge, so called because it drills tunnels into the coral's skeleton using an acid that dissolves the calcium carbonate. That can weaken the branch until it breaks. Red coral can also suffer from diseases, but all the natural causes of death are responsible for much less damage than human activities destroying it or changing its habitat. So now we need to protect it...

CORAL SKELETON DAMAGED
BY BORING SPONGE

A HAVEN
IN MARINE PROTECTED AREAS

IS RED CORAL AT RISK OF EXTINCTION?

Across the world, there are animals and plants that are at risk of going extinct if we don't do something to protect them. These all appear on the "red list of threatened species". The IUCN (International Union for Conservation of Nature) sets out the different levels of protection required, depending on how vulnerable the species is and the kind of threats it faces. Since 2014, red coral has been on the list, and it is classed as "endangered."

HOW CAN WE KEEP IT FROM DISAPPEARING?

Firstly, we need coral fishing practices to be more sustainable (see p. 38). We also need to protect coral from other threats, in safe places like marine protected areas, which are regulated and monitored. These well-preserved coral populations act as a reservoir. Little by little, the new corals born there can recolonize neighboring areas that have been depopulated.

WHERE ARE THESE SAFE HAVENS FOR CORAL?

Here, for example, in the Cerbère-Banyuls Marine Nature Reserve! It was established in 1974 and is one of the four oldest marine protected areas in the Mediterranean, along with the marine reserves in Carry-le-Rouet, Scandola in Corsica, and Spélugues in Monaco, which are also home to red coral. In this sanctuary, the coral has lived undisturbed for half a century and it has formed abundant colonies at depths of only around 20 meters! But it still hasn't grown to the size of some large specimens held in museums. Maybe in a few centuries, it will... The only people who are allowed access to this underwater treasure trove are scientists and, in some parts of the reserve, divers... as long as they are very careful!

The reserve often hosts researchers. Last week, it was Carine, a biology student researching red coral skeletons. But there are lots of other aspects of coral to study. **If you'd like to find out more, go and see her in her lab!** ▶

NAME: CARINE
JOB: RESEARCH STUDENT
LOCATION: MONACO
SCIENTIFIC CENTER

UNDERSTANDING MORE THROUGH **RESEARCH**

WHAT IS THE POINT OF RESEARCH?

Researchers want to know more about the living species that share our planet! So we carry out research to find out about red coral, how colonies develop, and what are the best conditions for it to grow in. These scientific findings help us to protect it more effectively, as they inform conservation measures, for example. They also help to raise awareness among the general public about how important this treasure is. And then, sometimes, a researcher gets unexpected results which lead to new avenues of research...

WHAT INTERESTING DISCOVERIES HAVE WE MADE?

We now know that there are surprising similarities between how red coral's calcium carbonate skeleton is created and how human teeth and bones are formed. Researchers are exploring ideas about how we could apply that to medicine in the future: how we could draw inspiration from coral to repair broken bones more effectively, use it for bone grafts, and maybe, one day, create artificial bones in a lab. We have also discovered that red coral contains a protein that is good for human skin, which has given scientists ideas for innovations in cosmetics. By doing more research, we may discover other useful properties that we can use in medicines.

WHY DO WE STUDY CORAL SKELETONS?

It allows us to see how aspects of the environment, such as the temperature or composition of sea water, have changed over time, because the mineral skeleton "records" these characteristics when it is formed. The growth rings in coral (see p. 23) are like archives storing information about the environment and the planet's climate over the last few centuries.

WILL IT ALSO RECORD CLIMATE CHANGE?

Of course. Experiments have also shown that ocean acidification, due to increased levels of carbon dioxide (CO_2) in the atmosphere, will cause its calcium carbonate skeleton to form more slowly (see p. 31).

Knowing more about coral has helped us to regulate coral fishing, for example. When I was your age, I used to go on vacation to Bonifacio in Corsica. I spent hours down at the harbor with Éric, a coral fisher who is passionate about his work. **If you go and find him, he'll tell you all about it!** ▶

NAME: ÉRIC
JOB: CORAL FISHER
LOCATION: BONIFACIO, CORSICA

SUSTAINABLE CORAL FISHING
FOR THE FUTURE

HOW DO YOU FISH FOR CORAL?

We use a depth sounder and a GPS to locate places where coral might be living, at depths of 80 meters or more, then we dive using scuba gear that recycles the air we breathe out. The "harvesting" takes around twenty minutes. We only harvest coral from large colonies, breaking pieces off with a small hammer. We leave the smaller ones so they can keep growing. Because of decompression sickness, which can sometimes be fatal if you're diving at great depths, it is a dangerous job.

CAN ANYONE BECOME A CORAL FISHER?

Nowadays coral harvesting is highly regulated. Everything is restricted and monitored: the quantity and size of the coral you harvest, the locations and times when you are allowed to do it (four months of the year), the depth (at least 50 meters), and even the number of coral fishers: in France, there are only 23 licenced professional coral fishers. All that is restrictive but it's necessary to make sure this precious resource doesn't run out. And that is in the interest of everyone who makes their living from red coral!

WHAT DID PEOPLE DO BEFORE SCUBA DIVING WAS INVENTED?

When lots of coral grew in shallow waters, people simply dived by holding their breath, as we can see from ancient carvings of fishing scenes. Then people started to use a device called a St. Andrew's Cross, which damaged the sea floor for centuries! It was a big wooden cross with weights and nets attached, operated by people on board a coral fishing boat, and it "blindly" ripped coral up from the bottom of the sea... along with anything else it found there! Around 1800, there were hundreds of these boats in the Kingdom of Naples! This type of fishing is very destructive and old-fashioned, and it was made illegal in 1994. From 1950 onwards, scuba diving revolutionized coral fishing. Luckily for us!

Lots of the coral we harvest is sent to Torre del Greco, near Naples, in Italy. It's the global capital of red coral jewelry and carving! **If you'd like to know more about what happens there, go and see Romie. She is jewelry maker, and she'll show you how it's done!** ▶

GLEAMING RED CORAL IN ART AND JEWELRY

NAME: ROMIE
JOB: JEWELRY MAKER
LOCATION: TORRE DEL GRECO, ITALY

? HOW DID TORRE DEL GRECO BECOME FAMOUS FOR RED CORAL?

Making jewelry and works of art from red coral has always been an important part of Mediterranean culture. From the twelfth century onward, Marseilles and Genoa, a busy port city in Italy, were the main coral carving centers. Thousands of people there made their living from the "red gold" industry. Then, the coral industry in Torre del Greco started up in the sixteenth century, and the town became world-famous for coral carving. Here, we've been in the coral industry for many generations!

WHAT HAPPENS TO CORAL AFTER IT IS HARVESTED?

When the raw coral arrives at the workshop, first we have to soak it in diluted bleach to remove the tissue from the hard, red skeleton (see p. 23). We sort the branches according to their size, color, and purity. We cut them into sections using a circular saw, holding them under a trickle of water so they don't break. Then the artist carefully carves the coral and polishes it. It's a bit like being at the dentist, as we use very similar instruments!

WHAT DO PEOPLE MAKE WITH CORAL?

Some artists, like the famous sculptor Carlo Parlati, specialize in carving little statues from pieces of coral. You have to be very skilled and creative to do that! Red coral can also be made into beautiful beads for necklaces, and all sorts of jewelry and pendants, which are often inspired by the natural shape of the branch. But coral doesn't just appear in jewelry shop windows! In Tibet and Mongolia, it is considered holy and used to decorate masks and costumes for religious rituals. It is also found in the traditional jewelry of certain groups in Africa.

Would you prefer to admire red coral in its natural habitat? You are like my friend Capucine. She's a diver, naturalist, and keen underwater photographer. **Go and see her for me. She's having an exhibition of her photos in Naples at the moment!** ▶

NAME: CAPUCINE
JOB: NATURE PHOTOGRAPHER
LOCATION: NAPLES, ITALY

A CORNERSTONE OF BIODIVERSITY

TUBEWORM

YELLOW GORGONIAN

ANEMONES

SPONGE

? WHAT IS A NATURE PHOTOGRAPHER?

It's someone who combines their passion for photography with an interest in nature. You have to do a lot of research so you know all about the living species you're observing. I even have a third passion: scuba diving! I often take photos of red coral and the colorful little world around it. We call this the "coralligenous" and it is only found in the Mediterranean.

WHAT IS THE CORALLIGENOUS MADE UP OF?

It's a densely populated community of animals and algae that live together in the same habitat as red coral. Sponges, tubeworms, anemones, small corals, gorgonians, encrusting algae: they cover the entire surface of the rock, leaving no empty space!

IS CORAL USEFUL FOR OTHER SPECIES?

It is very important because of its shape.
Like the trees in a forest, its branches create
a three-dimensional world in which lots of species
of fish and crustaceans can shelter! We call it an
"engineer." It plays an important role in increasing
biodiversity—the number of different species.
Without it, some of them wouldn't be there.

AND IS IT IMPORTANT FOR US TOO?

Of course, even if we don't hide in it! It is important
simply because it is beautiful and fascinating, and
that makes us want to look more closely at it. That's
what I try to show in my photos. The sense of
amazement we feel when we see so much beauty at
the heart of nature is very important, because that is
what we need to feel to protect our planet and all its
living species.

ENCRUSTING
ALGAE

Here, take this photo. I took it six years
ago. The coral will probably be a bit
bigger now!

STILL SO MANY MYSTERIES TO EXPLORE

Summer was over. Back at Granny's house, I felt a bit sad because
I'd come to the end of my investigation so soon. I flicked through
my notebook and stuck the photo that Capucine had given me
on the cover. I looked at it for a long time. The summer break had
never gone by so fast. And it had never been so exciting!
I had solved the mystery of the red coral. At least... some of it.
But it is still very mysterious. Even my researcher and biologist
friends don't know everything about it! Each person secretly
told me a question that science still hasn't been able to answer.
Why does it grow so slowly compared to other corals? Why is it red?
Why do the polyps tend to come out at night? Why do the larvae
attach themselves to rocks?
So... that means I can carry on with my investigation!
In the meantime, I've drawn a map of my journey studying the red
gold of the Mediterranean. You can see my itinerary and all the people
I talked to. And if you like, you can carry on researching too!

SOMMAIRE

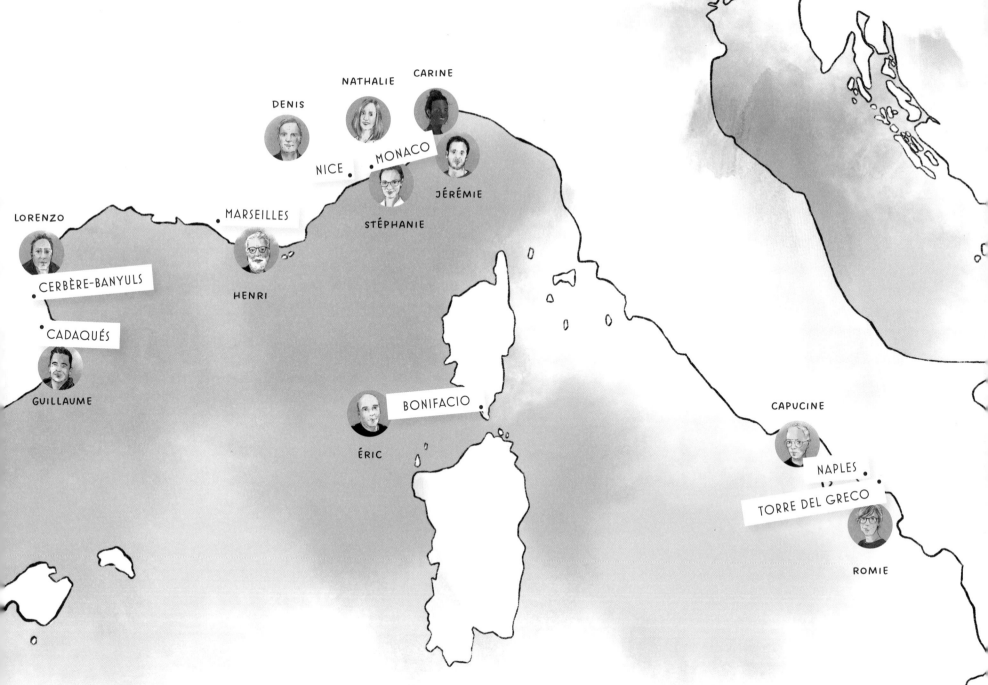